CREATIVE THINKING
for the
21st CENTURY:
AN EXPERIENTIAL GUIDEBOOK

By Sandy Sims, in collaboration with Dr. Kerry Monick, M.D.

Creative Thinking for the 21st Century: An Experiential Guidebook

Global Creative Thinking Institute LLC, Publisher
220 N. Zapata Hwy 11, Suite 642B
Laredo, TX 78043-4464 U.S.A.
sandersonsims@gmail.com

ISBN: 978-0-9827457-0-0
LCCN: 2010-908565

For orders of more than twenty books please contact the publisher.

CREATIVE THINKING for the 21st CENTURY: AN EXPERIENTIAL GUIDEBOOK

About This Workbook — A Note from Sandy Sims

My book, *How Frank Lloyd Wright Got Into My Head, Under My Skin And Changed The Way I Think About Thinking: A Creative Thinking Blueprint for the 21st Century*, is a book about self-discovery. I describe how in the first half of my life I was not conscious of forces that were aligned with me, and how in the second half I became aware of these same forces and tested them.

Yet, as we all know, it is one thing to know how to do something, and quite another to implement with practice and training until results confirm something and make it a part of our belief system.

There are countless books and motivational programs to inspire and cajole us. Yet just as in sports, we must first become reasonably fit as a precursor to believing that we can excel. This is a bio-feedback loop: we work out, muscles appear, our endurance increases, and we gain confidence in our ability to improve and perform at higher levels. It is a continuous process.

I maintain that consciousness development is exactly the same. We can be told that we create our own reality, or that we can overcome our fears. But until we gain a certain grounding in who we really are — that is, understand how the hardware that is "us" operates best, and understand the full potential of how the software that guides us functions — we are limited.

Aside from learning about our capabilities, there is the context of the times in which we live. Technology is compressing time, pushing decision-making to the last moments. This is forcing the conscious development and use of our intuitive skills. The luxury of time for endless examination is disappearing. The emergence of social media is instantly revealing the truth about products and services. Transparency is becoming the new norm in business. Old lifestyle models of enduring dreary jobs for the pot of gold at retirement are over. The promise of the rewards of older retirement lifestyles is not holding up. Additionally the world's entire financial model has been turned upside down. Savings have disappeared. We are at a watershed.

To cope, we are learning from quantum physics about how the universe at the atomic level is alive and interconnected. What the mystics could not explain but knew to be true, the scientists are slowly discovering; they are accepting that "absence of proof is not proof of absence."

We seem to be powerful processors and transmitters sending thought patterns with varying degrees of force (intent and emotion) that code and organize energy to instantly respond and align with the thought being sent. Of course there are other transmitters (people) sending out creative code, some in opposition to us. What finally materializes is a function of complexity, of sympathetic and opposing forces. To make matters more provocative I have proposed that we have access to levels of conscious beings in realms we cannot see, but with whom we can and do partner. For example where does a completely new and novel idea come from? What about intuition? Where does a hunch come from? I like to think of these as incoming messages from other realms that are aligned with us, messages that our individual and particular software receives and interprets.

To operate efficiently within this system, think of having rules of engagement or code.

The purpose of this workbook is to examine the operating system of "our equipment" from this perspective.

To help you along, I am going to review my journey of discovery, underlining the sections that shaped my belief system. Look at parallels in your own life and see where they fit for you.

Sandy's Review, Part One: The Unconscious Phase

I grew up in a middle class family during the '50s. My father and mother separated, which was not typical for that period. My mother went back to college in her forties. She was independent. My grandfather was a wealthy entrepreneur who had been bankrupt twice before real estate paid off. My father was an Ivy League graduate who wanted to be a journalist, but not enough to break the family demands that he stay close to home and join the family business.

My environment was filled with hope and optimism. World War II had ended. People were seeking the good life — buying appliances, cars, and homes. Growing up also meant preparing for a profession and studying hard, because education was the springboard to a better life. My father drilled into me that the better I did in school the better my life would be. He made sure I understood that being broke was a terrible life, one to be avoided at all costs. He would point at manual laborers and warn me that I could end up like them if I didn't knuckle down. From this point of view, fear of what could happen was a great motivator. At the core, my family members were products of the Protestant Work Ethic: you could have whatever you wanted if you worked hard enough for it. A little luck would definitely help. We were not religious. Yet there was strong sense of moral values. I was a Cub Scout, Boy Scout, even an Eagle Scout, Little Leaguer, and on athletic teams in high school. I was normal. In my final year at Emory University, a Methodist-denominated school, I remember my comparative religion professor deducing that one must simply have faith, because events like the Holocaust were simply unexplainable. I was not satisfied with that answer. It had no utility. But I didn't know how or where to get better information. So I accepted it.

My friends were products of the same values. We were college-bound, because that was what you did. Becoming a medical or legal professional, working for a large corporation, joining a family business… these were the paths that seemed natural. Our parents seemed to know best and we did what we were told. The world around us told us this was true. Furthermore if we worked hard we could save and then retire to a golden period of "whatever we wanted to do."

I was not a brilliant student, but a reasonable plodder; if I studied, a "B" was in sight, but "As" were much harder to acquire. I clicked with people, and had a flair for design. I would work hard if I could find the right endeavor. I kept my antennae up, constantly scanning to see what was working for whom. My uncles were government workers. Their lives looked safe but boring. I felt a little luck would be helpful, but I couldn't count on it. Deep inside the need to be an entrepreneur haunted me, but I dreaded the test.

Since my father's career path had been cut short by his fear that his mother and father would disown him if he strayed too far afield from the family development business, he never followed his own deep desires. He wanted me to succeed for both of us. As a result, I was happy to find ways to keep from getting started. There was the military obligation, then graduate school. In fact I used up the entire decade of my twenties putting things off.

As my life unfolded in college a classroom professor talked about finding a place you really wanted to live and building your life from there as an option to taking the first job offer and going where that took you. His message was that you would feel partially successful in life immediately and it wouldn't matter what you had done. I finished college, and then met a resort bartender who told me about how he ran a Navy officer's club in Roto, Spain. To do so I would need a second bachelor's degree, one in Hotel and Restaurant management. Florida State University, in my hometown, had such a program. The local draft board gave me a deferment and I followed the same path to Navy Officer Candidate School, and then to managing clubs. In OCS I had several close calls that could have washed me out. The company commander seemed to look out for me. He was in love with my Volkswagen. I graduated and sold it to him. I felt lucky about this whole turn of events.

In the Navy I was sent to Hawaii. Getting off the plane on Oahu and smelling those fragrant plumerias I knew Honolulu would be "that place" the college professor had talked about. But shortly thereafter I was transferred to the Island of Hawaii to a military vacation camp in Hawaii Volcanoes National Park. For me it was in the middle of nowhere. I wanted out in the worst way, writing endless letters to the Bureau of Naval Personnel. Finally they responded and sent me to Japan in return for an additional year of service. Yet during that period the main volcanic caldera erupted, as did numerous other sites in the park. It was a once-in-a-century spectacle. I *was living in the center of it.*

After the Navy, I returned home to Tallahassee with hepatitis. I stayed at home and enrolled in graduate business school. I was thinking mostly in terms of getting the degree as an insurance policy, for a fallback teaching qualification, in case life dealt me a bad hand. I was not there for the love of learning, yet I was intrigued with one course called "Techniques of Financial Analysis." I naively signed up, not realizing it was required for a Ph.D. There were only ten or so students.

Making a D- on the midterm I realized I would flunk out if I didn't pass this course. I ground out thirty study hours a week on this one course, passed the final exam and survived graduate school. I had learned a profoundly useful skill: how to analyze and finance a small business.

Finally it was my moment of truth: with MBA in hand, I bought a one-way ticket to Hawaii. After interviewing with many people, the Bank of Hawaii offered me a job in the credit analysis department. I was sick to my stomach. I couldn't do it. I turned it down, only to find a teaching position for the school year in a junior college.

During that year I designed a coupon book to sell to the Japanese. After four months, I made my presentation, but failed miserably. They liked the idea, but didn't want to pay me. Yet the process had introduced me to two advertising creative stars that were opening an ad agency and needed a manager and account man.

A year later the partners had a falling out and I joined the writer. Honolulu had not needed another advertising agency, much less two. I implored my dad to put up some money. It was a struggle. <u>I felt we could fail at any time. I didn't know how to handle that kind of failure. Unknowingly I was worrying myself into a breakdown. I felt I had to succeed for both Dad and myself</u>. I collapsed with a relapse of hepatitis. It was 1972 and I was 30 years old.

To this stage I can summarize my belief system like this:

- *I very much depended on linear thinking. Plan, work, save, take calculated risks, and hope for the best. The harder I worked the more I could insure against an unsure future.*

- *Strong fears existed around failure. My father had been afraid to stand on his own two feet, and that had not given me a great deal of confidence.*

- *Good luck and bad luck were random events. Fate was an arbitrary mistress.*

- *The way the world operated beyond these beliefs was not on my radar screen. Spiritually I felt that if I practiced the "Golden Rule," that would be good enough, but I wasn't going to count on anything to solve challenges. My mother had read to me Aesop's Fables and fairy tales as a preschool youngster. These had suggested to me that being a decent human being would make life less complicated, but that I couldn't count on any divine help to rescue me from life's scrapes.*

- *I looked at what was working for people who had my skills and background, and decided to model myself on them.*

- *I was striving to be my own person, be adventuresome to a degree, and not settle or sell myself out.*

Even being a product of some privilege, I was anxious, fearful, and unsure. I had a certain amount of courage, but had brought myself to the breaking point with inner torment, rendering myself physically unable to continue.

In desperation one day, while driving the car back from half-days at the office to collapse into bed, with the windows up I screamed with all of the energy I could muster, "I need help."

A week later a friend called, inviting me to accept a blind date. Kerry, a pert, attractive blond surgeon-turned-psychiatrist entered my life. We became an item for the next two years. My scream seemed to have summoned forces to give me just the help I required. I needed an expanded point of view, one that would awaken me to the larger reality in which I was living, but of which I was unaware.

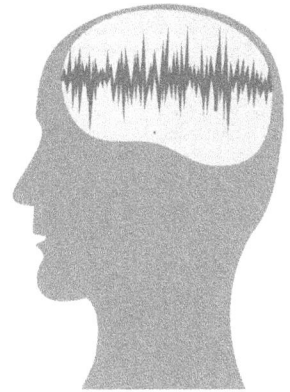

Learning More: A Review of Your Life

The first part of your personal journey is to examine what you believe to be true. See if you can uncover the origins of your self-beliefs, how they have tracked over time, and what they are now.

Write a short review of your own life.

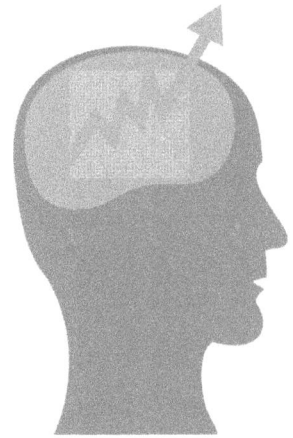

Learning More: An Inventory of How You Feel Now

Take inventory of yourself, your main core drivers. Ask yourself these questions.

What do I believe about how things work? What do I count on?

What are my fears?

Am I doing what I really like? If not, what are the obstacles in my way?

Am I happy? If not, what am I unhappy about?

What have been the big breaks and setbacks in my life?

What have been major turning points?

What do I want that has not happened?

Now answer these questions about this exercise.

What have I learned from this exercise?

Where are my opportunities?

What actions will I take?

Sandy's Review, Part Two: The Awakening Phase

*E*arly *in our relationship, Kerry asked me one night if I had ever thought my brain was being shared with another person somewhere else on the planet. I was intrigued. She then took it a few steps further and suggested for consideration that our paired brains might be part of a larger brain comprised of six pairs, and this larger brain to an even larger brain. Eventually it became clear where this was going. The exercise triggered a profound change in me, not one I initiated consciously. It was as if a switch clicked on in my brain. My appetite had been whetted for more information. Suddenly I was curious. I was thirsty for more ideas like this one.*

Kerry suggested that I start by reading some of the works of Vera Stanley Alder. Vera would be an easy introduction to metaphysics. Born in the last days of the 19th century, Vera was a distant cousin to Niels Bohr, a Nobel Prize winner for physics. A successful painter, she had a gift of tying together social progress, technology and mystic spirituality. Her books were easy and thought-provoking — kind of a baby pabulum approach — filled with tidbits such as, "Why do ice crystals form in the shape of fern leaves?" Next were the books by Jane Roberts on the entity called "Seth" that she channeled. If you have ever wondered what listening to a mind with an IQ of 400 would be like, this was it. I was hooked. I was resonating with concepts I had never even begun to imagine. One of the central tenets was the profound idea that we human beings "create our own reality" by what we think and want. We also draw to us what we fear.

There, of course are the skeptics, whose main contention is that proof of mystical ideas are lacking and therefore are quackery. Yet frequently the skeptic has merely suggested that since there is no science to prove these claims, then they must be false. But just because we have no proof does not mean that a phenomenon does not exist.

Today the gap between science and mysticism is narrowing. The Field, *by Lynne McTaggart, and her follow-up book,* The Intention Experiment, *begin to connect the dots in this area.*

Quantum physicist and Princeton doctoral candidate, Hugh Everett III, proposed that we have parallel universes in which various events such as wars have different outcomes in these interconnected worlds. There are movies like What the Bleep Do We Know? *and its sequel,* Down the Rabbit Hole, *which reveal to us these mind-boggling quantum physics connections between our minds and what happens as a consequence of how we use them. The entire universe appears to be alive and interconnected. Now we are finding out just how.*

I did not care about whether information was channeled or not, proven or not; I was interested in checking it out for myself. If our thoughts with intention created reality, I wanted to see for myself.

Kerry and I began our own little experiments. We would intentionally want a parking place in a specific location and then notice whether it appeared as we drove up. Not every time, but frequently it did. Elevator doors began to open more often than not. People we had been thinking about would show up on chance encounters. I began to review my past. What had I really wanted? Had it shown up? When? If it didn't happen, what might have been the opposing forces aligned against it? After all, we were sharing this space with many others, wanting exactly the same outcome — like wanting to win a lottery. Were we in a grander scheme beyond our thoughts and imagination?

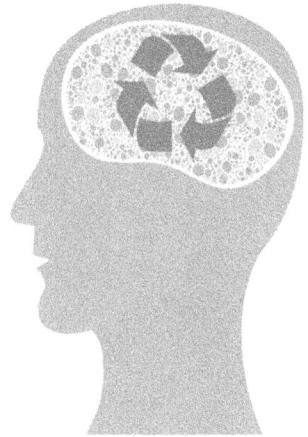

Learning More: Conscious Manifestation

Think back over the last several months, or even longer periods, about conditions, events, people, and outcomes you wanted to bring to your reality. Write down as many as you can remember. <u>It doesn't matter how simple the ideas were: the goal is to see the pattern and bring this into your consciousness</u>. For example, let's say you told yourself you would really like to meet a particular person. Several years later you treated yourself to a business class seat, and sitting next to you or across the aisle was that very person. This happens all of the time to everybody. Yet, we write it off to coincidence or luck, or if it is too "insignificant," to nothing at all.

<u>When you write down enough of these, you will see that YOU have been the architect and creator, and these desires have transpired because you wanted them to</u>. In the Seth material, Seth says that we live in multiple frameworks. In our framework a desire sends an order. In another framework this order summons legions of energetic forces to deliver it.

On the next pages, try to list up to eight such desires that finally materialized. Briefly describe the desire, the approximate date you wanted it, and when it happened. Describe the nature of the outcome. If you need more space, turn to the back of the workbook and expand your thoughts there. Be sure to note the lag time — the time it takes for a desire to manifest itself. Sometimes the lag time is so great we don't see the connection to the original desire.

1.

2.

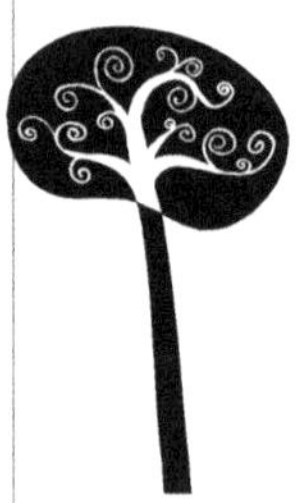

3.

4.

5.

6.

7.

8.

What kind of changes do you feel when you acknowledge that this collection of manifestations occurred? Do you see a pattern? Does it feel like there is inter-connectedness? If yes, describe it.

Answer yes, no, or not sure. Do you feel:

- A little more powerful, but certainly not willing to risk too much?

- A little more powerful and curious to consciously connect future desires to outcomes and lag times?

- Anxious to learn more about the factors affecting outcomes before you place more faith in the process?

- Confident and willing to test this with more at risk?

Now answer these questions about this exercise.

What have I learned from this exercise?

Where are my opportunities?

What actions will I take?

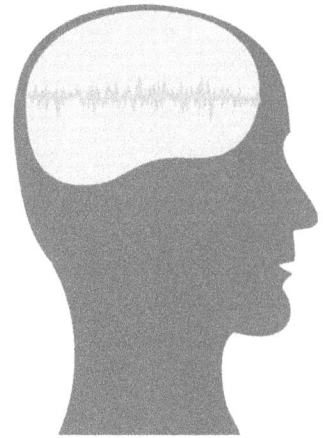

Learning More: Stronger Opposing Forces

The purpose of this exercise is to recognize that failure does not imply lack of creative power on your part, but is an indicator that a greater opposing force was in play. It may not just be an opposing person but a larger dynamic such as a social condition or movement.

For example, if you are speeding in a residential neighborhood and get caught by a policeman, it is the desire of the residents collectively that speeding be stopped.

Perhaps the desire is of such large magnitude that you doubt it could occur. *Most people who buy a lottery ticket don't expect to win. Perhaps too much opposition tends to shut us down. We doubt our power and may feel a lack of confidence and low self-esteem.*

When he was growing up, Sandy's parents often promised him a pony. He never got one. Obviously they didn't want a pony around or its responsibility. Their desire was in opposition to his.

Think of up to eight strong desires which did not occur. See if you can identify the opposing force.

1.

2.

3.

4.

5.

6.

7.

8.

Do you still feel as powerful as you did before this exercise? Describe your feelings.

If you feel less powerful, take some time. Think of several more positive desires that came into existence. How does this make you feel?

Now answer these questions about this exercise.

What have I learned from this exercise?

Where are my opportunities?

What actions will I take?

Sandy's Review, Part Three: Reinforcement

*A*s time went by I began to apply what I was learning to my business. I wanted to see it grow and do well. I didn't know how, but I could accept and believe that forces were at work on my behalf.

I began to credit myself for things I had previously been oblivious to.

- *I had wanted to go to college. I did.*

- *I had wanted to find an elegant way to deal with my military obligation. I did.*

- *I had wanted to live in paradise. I did — Hawaii.*

- *I had wanted to succeed as an entrepreneur at something I was suited to within a desired environment. This was a long process. Follow the thread. I wanted to employ my talents, which were counseling and aesthetics. Unknowingly I had needed some skills furnished by the finance course in business school. What resulted (manifested, in this new terminology) was an advertising agency in Hawaii.*

I had desperately wanted help. I was still being driven by old values and had lost my health. I had been unconsciously manifesting but because I wasn't aware of my true part, I still was being driven by old values. I had made myself sick. The resulting events, catalyzed by Kerry, opened me to a new way of perceiving.

As I studied and practiced I began to accept <u>and believe</u> that I was a creator in this sense, albeit not a big one. I was now convinced that I was more responsible for how things were working than were just chance and good luck. My desires, intentions and dedication had produced results. I was beginning to accept that there was a larger order, one I needed to learn much more about.

One of the books I had bought and read was Paul Hawken's The Magic of Findhorn. *Peter Caddy, who was a cofounder of Findhorn, had been a Royal Air Force catering officer.*

He, together with Eileen, left the Officer Corps of the Royal Air Force to follow her spiritual guidance. They made a pact: she would receive the guidance, and he, unquestioningly, and no matter how absurd it seemed at the time, would carry out her orders. From a desolate sandy plot in Scotland evolved the magical gardens of Findhorn where gigantic vegetables were raised and roses grew out of the snow. They had connected with the nature spirits and the gardens were a demonstration. But more important to me was the concept of what their vision was: to show people a new way to think and to manifest. The Caddys had virtually nothing, but as they needed resources of any kind, these resources would show up. Slowly the gardens and community flourished, and they became both a world novelty and a center for this new way of thinking.

I had been lying on the couch one night, reading Hawken's book and realized how much I wanted to meet Peter — really meet him. We both had similar backgrounds in the military, and he had stepped into an entirely new world. I admired his courage. I thought about how much I wanted to meet him. I let the idea go. The agency was now prospering, and I was incorporating some of these principles into my daily life. Time slipped by.

Charlie Campbell, who was a partner in our Frank Lloyd Wright Collection project, called me one afternoon. He said he had a friend who was coming to Honolulu and needed a place to stay. I gave it no thought, saying, "Sure send him over."

At 8:00 p.m. that evening there was a loud knock on the door. I opened it. An outstretched hand powerfully gripped mine. "Peter Caddy. Glad to meet you," he said. I was stunned.

My mind seized upon one thing: two years! That had been the time lapse between my reading The Magic of Findhorn, wanting to meet Peter, and his showing up at my front door. The lag time is so important because as the lag time increases, one's belief tends to decrease. Too many events conspire to muddy the waters.

My curiosity was now fully engaged. Here was my mentor. Peter and I spent the entire week together, and I had the chance to learn first-hand his experiences using this discipline. Later David Caddy, their son, would come and live with me for three months, and while he was there, his mother Eileen would visit.

Upon reflection, their personal appearance in my life reinforced a whole new way of being in me. They were not so much interested in people coming to Findhorn to live, but in people seizing these ideas and putting them into practice.

One of the exercises at Findhorn was to teach people "the laws of manifestation." They would be sent to the European continent with only $50 in their pockets and told to return in six weeks with their stories. They were to surrender to the universe with the idea that they would be taken care of. Peter, Eileen and David made sure I heard those stories.

In summary, the guiding principles were:

- *Having a pure thought from the heart. (We like to think of this as creating the blueprint of an order to be issued.)*

- *Having desire and intention as the delivery system.*

- *Reveling in the feeling of its being done.*

- *Releasing and thanking the forces of the universe in advance, <u>knowing and trusting</u> that these forces would deliver if the order were in proper alignment with supportive conditions.*

Supportive conditions were still a puzzle. There are countless people whose desires are at play all of the time, some in alignment with you and some against. In the case of the Findhorn students sent out to trust the universe for six weeks, their order was far-ranging: it said "take care of me anyway that you can."

If you have a singleness of purpose — such as a desire to be a great actor or athlete or, for that matter, anything of great accomplishment — you may feel these forces are aligned with you, yet you are in a competitive arena. The process will no doubt be long and arduous, but breaks and good fortune will occur because as you succeed your <u>belief strengthens</u> and the supportive forces in the background are working to deliver.

<u>There still is room for confusion.</u> Years ago I went to see the legendary Mother Meara in Germany. People were coming to her from all over the world to participate in her silent darshan sessions. In the library room was one of her books. As I thumbed through it I found a section on questions. A fellow had said that his passion was piccolo playing. He had a wife and two children. He was confused because he wanted the universe to support his family solely from his piccolo playing. His question to Mother Meara was, "Can I trust the universe to take care of me in this endeavor?" Her reply to him was, "Don't give up your day job." As a single person, perhaps he could have scraped by playing his musical instrument. But he had raised the ante.

He had created a family. His new responsibilities required that he give up something in return, at least in the short run. Were he — through diligent practice, performances etc. — to become known, then perhaps sufficient funds would come in to support the family.

Learning More: Reinforcement

Get a journal. Write some of big desires you have had in your life that have not occurred. Note the date that you first had these desires. Be sure to record the small things that you have wanted also. They will show up much sooner. When anything shows up, note the date, what happened, the lag time and how you feel.

Now answer these questions about this exercise.

What have I learned from this exercise?

Where are my opportunities?

What actions will I take?

Refining the Process

We have discussed having a thought that becomes a heart's desire with intention, and a belief that it will happen. Not only can there be opposition, but your thoughts and desires may be too haphazard, too fuzzy. A common expression we have all heard says, "Be careful of what you want because you may get it."

There is a very cute movie, released not too long ago, called *Bedazzled*. Elizabeth Hurley plays the devil and Elliot Richards plays a geeky dork working in a dead-end job in a San Francisco call center. He has no friends and his associates manipulate him for their amusement. In this particular movie, the geeky dork has desperately fallen for a young woman, Allison, who won't have anything to do with him. Because he feels powerless to win her over, he makes a pact with devil to create what he cannot do for himself. The devil sells him seven wishes in exchange for his soul. This follows the age-old "deal with the devil" known as the "Faustian bargain," after the German legend of Faust.

Immediately our dork tells the devil that he wants to be rich and powerful and he wants to be married to Allison. He wakes up to find himself a rich Latin American drug lord embroiled in all kinds of struggles. As he looks out the window of his mansion he sees Allison, who detests him, in the arms of a lover. Our geeky dork is furious and pushes the red-buttoned escape device to return. The devil reminds him that he received exactly what he asked for, to be rich, powerful and married to Allison. In frustration he subsequently uses up his wishes asking to be sensitive, then a super athlete, then well endowed, then president of the United States. Each time he is given what he wants only to find that he is undone by what he cannot imagine.

The Faustian bargain is much closer to reality than we sometimes like to think. We strongly desire something and work hard to get it, only to find out in the end that obtaining it did not bring the satisfaction we were seeking. We often want things to show others that we are successful and will practically kill ourselves to get them. Yet what we wanted may have been what we thought those things would bring, e.g. happiness, a sense of well being, peace of mind, etc. <u>Could we have gotten there another way?</u>

What We Should Want

In the beginning we are searching for evidence of our creative power. Of course we need the necessities of life, and more than that, a certain amount of comfort, security and those things which support our individuality. Abraham Maslow is famous for identifying our "hierarchy of needs," with survival requirements at the bottom of the pyramid and self-actualization at the top. We need to connect our desires with manifestation. Once we see this connection, the challenge becomes figuring how to use these powers to truly make our life rewarding and exhilarating.

If we accept that our journey is to learn how to master our creative power, which is what this guidebook is about, then creating a lot of unnecessary things in our life is like dragging a sea anchor behind a small sailboat.

Recognizing that we have these powers and seeking answers to questions might be the first logical step. Tony Robbins and other "New Thought" leaders have expressed the point this way: the quality of our lives is determined by the questions we ask.

There are many popular books suggesting ways to use your creative power to make a million dollars, or to become financially independent, or to work only a few hours a week so you can go do what you want to do. Our only comment is that if you love, for example, doing deals — and this is a passion that makes your heart sing — then you know it is right for you. The money that comes with it is a by-product. However, working seventy to eighty hours a week, or even four hours, for that matter, at something you don't want to do, is a recipe for burnout. You may not be in the perfect space at this moment, but by identifying the most useful questions, you will be on the right path.

If you turn your question into a demand, into an order, with belief and intent, then you are creating an order. There may be lag time, but you can count on receiving an answer. Your question does not oppose anyone else. If you demand to know what your purpose is, then nothing will prevent you from acquiring the answer. It may come in a multitude of forms, such as picking up the right book, or meeting the right person. Maybe the answer will come from a movie, a television program, or a conversation. Maybe it will come from a sudden insight. It doesn't matter. <u>You will know because you will feel relieved by that piece of information.</u> Like a stepping-stone, it will lead you to that next opportunity, relationship, or event that will ultimately make your life's journey more rewarding.

Here's an example: about midway into Sandy's career as the president of his advertising agency, he came into the office one morning at 8:30 to find that he had fifteen phone calls waiting for him. In short, he was overwhelmed. He knew he needed to make some changes. He was still handling key accounts and was accessible to everyone.

He went home that weekend, sat down with a journal, and wrote out three ways he wanted to spend a day in the office; three ways he wanted to spend a weekend day; and three ways he wanted to spend a holiday. None of them featured fifteen phone calls waiting for his response first thing in the morning. In fact, his ideal office day had virtually no incoming phone calls — save social invitations.

He put the journal away and forgot about it. Several years later, he was rummaging though some files in his home office and found the journal. He opened it and, to his utter amazement, realized that he was living the kind of days he had described a few years before.

At that moment he could not even recall all the changes that had transpired. Yet that initial act had begun the process.

Learning More: Redefining Your Creative Orders As Feelings

No matter where on the journey you are, it may be much more important to know the right road to travel than to know what's at the end of it.

For example, if you feel pulled toward a certain profession, place to live, or hobby, you can move with enthusiasm, not knowing where it might lead or what it might bring to you. This in no way negates goals. It just says that your goal is a feeling, and whatever is produced as a result of obtaining those feelings is good enough.

If you have a clear vision of something you want to build or own for the sheer joy of it, the feeling is the same. Your goal is pure experience, a feeling you want to have. Eliminate the intermediate goal of what you think will bring you that feeling. Concentrate on the feeling itself.

The Oracle at Delphi contains two inscriptions as advice to mankind. "Know Thyself" and "Nothing in Excess." Perhaps it will take a lifetime to know yourself, but with practice and thought you will be able to shape the more important questions.

These can be expressed as demands, eventually giving you answers and directions for an optimum life.

Think of a goal or an unfulfilled desire that you may have at the moment. See if you can identify the underlying feeling.

For example, "I want three million dollars because it will make me feel secure." Or, "I want a bigger house because it will make me feel successful."

Or, "I want to be a member of a club because it will make me feel accepted." Or, "I want to own a hybrid car because it will show that I am a conscious person doing my part." Or, "I want to get out of the city to a place in the country to give me a sense of relaxed pace and community."

Now, describe these goals.

I want _____ because it will make me feel

_____.

I want _____ because it will make me feel

_____.

I want _____ because it will make me feel

_____.

I want _____ because it will make me feel

_____.

I want _____ because it will make me feel

_____.

Now go back to the statements you made, eliminate the intermediate objects of desire, and change them to a command about how you want to feel.

For example if you wrote, "I want to have three million dollars because it will make me feel secure," change it to, "I demand to feel secure."

Other examples might be:

- *I demand to feel joy.*
- *I demand to feel happiness.*
- *I demand to feel connectedness.*
- *I demand to feel purposefulness.*
- *I demand to feel aliveness.*
- *I demand to feel graciousness.*
- *I demand to feel love.*

Feel the intensity behind your statement. Revel in what it feels like. Give thanks and let it go.

What you have done is to allow the universe maximum creativity in giving you what you want.

Will you suddenly feel what you asked for? Not likely. Will you begin to participate in confidence-building exercises, like the ones we are doing here, where you begin to sense your own power? Probably. In time you will know that no matter what happens to you, you have belief tools at hand to create what you require.

Now answer these questions about this exercise.

What have I learned from this exercise?

Where are my opportunities?

What actions will I take?

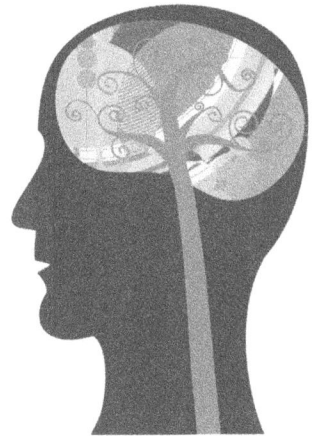

Learning More: Redefining Your Creative Orders As Pure Experiences

A pure experience might be:

- *I want to own a BMW to appreciate a finely made automobile.*

- *I want to take a trip to experience being immersed in another culture.*

- *I want to read this book to savor the words of James Allen.*

- *I want to dine at a 3-star Michelin restaurant to experience the art of gourmet cooking.*

- *I want to volunteer in a soup kitchen to feel a part of a community.*

- *I want to learn another language in order to have a richer experience of a culture.*

- *I want to run a marathon to see if I can.*

- *I want to learn more about my computer's capabilities so I can stay abreast of the changes in the world around me.*

Make a list of pure experiences you would like to have:

1.

2.

3.

4.

5.

6.

7.

8.

How do you feel about changing your ultimate desires to feelings and pure experiences? Does it feel more freeing? Does it feel more satisfying? What else?

Now answer these questions about this exercise.

What have I learned from this exercise?

What are my opportunities?

What actions will I take?

The Nature of the Field

Let's delve a bit deeper into the nature of the field that responds to our desires. We have reviewed how there is a fabric in our lives: one we heretofore have taken for granted as being random, coincidental, and not connected. For example:

- You were thinking about calling someone and at precisely that moment they phoned you, or you ran into them in the supermarket, in the parking lot or on the street.

- You needed some money in a hurry and a check from an unexpected source arrived in the mail.

- You were late for a critical meeting, but when you got there, thankfully the meeting was delayed a bit, so you were not late after all.

- You gave someone something to mail, only to find out that it wasn't necessary — and then learned that the person you gave it to forgot to mail it.

None of these things might look to have been related, but that is exactly what we have been examining.

Carl Jung referred to the collective unconscious as a repository for a multitude of connections that we as a culture are learning about and accepting. Rupert Sheldrake, the English biologist, has referred to morphogenetic fields as places where consciousness shares information. He has shown that where animals and birds learn patterns of behavior or how to accomplish a task, the entire species soon knows how to do this. The actual science behind this has not been explained yet, but physicists will no doubt uncover the quantum physics behind it.

"Absence of proof is not proof of absence." The skeptical world frequently cannot accept the reality of a phenomenon unless the science of it can be demonstrated.

Yet we are living in an accelerating time, one that asks us to trust more and more in outcomes just to survive. And as we do, we see that it can work. It is almost as if we are being asked to trust the process knowing that an explanation of the way it works will eventually follow.

We have already seen that an animal or a bird seems to acquire knowledge from the field; logic suggests it must work the same for human beings as well.

We have the further gift of self-examination. We are able to ask how this field works. From observation we have learned that the question itself creates an order or a command, either for an answer, or an action, or both. In this regard a desire is also an order. While we may not as yet have the science to explain the organizing principles, we have evidence that patterns of conscious thought and behavior produce intended results beyond coincidence or chance.

If you send an order to the universe with conviction, and that order is fulfilled, you don't have to understand the organizing principles to accept the results.

In Sandy's case he simply wanted to reduce this phenomenon down to a familiar scale. He wanted to think that he had helpers, playmates, or companions all willing to do his bidding. In his book he refers to them as Invisible Partners.

We all have Invisible Partners. The goal is to become aware of them, and to improve the communication between them and us in order to enhance our lives.

Sandy had to create a simple construct. He let his Partners know what he wanted. They made arrangements for those desires to manifest in the material world.

The "lack of signal," or confusion, issue

One of the most challenging issues is the perplexing issue of discerning the difference between an intuitive hit and a mental impulse. Frequently we want something so badly that we start tricking and confusing ourselves; there simply is not much energy around the situation. At the other end of the spectrum there is the signal that is so clear that you feel you simply "know" it is the right direction to take. In the former situation you may want to pair the decisions into two categories — consequential and inconsequential.

If the decision contains substantial consequences and you have time you may simply ask for a clearer signal and wait. If time is of the essence you may want to try other ways to make contact with your subconscious (see below). If it is truly a big decision and you feel blocked and not confident in the answers you are getting, take that as a "no." In other words, the confusion and doubt surrounding it is a vote for "no." This is the kind of situation that occurs, for example, when you are offered what looks like a great job or opportunity and you really want it because the idea of it looks so good. Yet, while you acknowledge that something is missing, you want it so badly that you don't want to accept any doubts.

Sometimes you may be weighing two poor decisions and wrestling over which one to make. No clear direction has energy because neither idea is good.

Other means to validate the subconscious and gain useful guidance

Because this is such a grey area with regard to desires we feel anxious about, there are other ways to connect with our subconscious, the collective unconscious, and our Invisible Partners.

For example you can use applied kinesiology, a muscle-testing process that uses your own biofeedback system to gain insight. Holding your arm out in front of you, have someone else ask you a question while applying downward pressure on your arm. A truthful answer will produce concurrent strength: your arm will have the energy to resist and stay pointing outward. With a false answer your arm will easily be pushed downward.

Truth is processed in this manner because the body is an electrical field. Advanced researchers, such as David R. Hawkins, M.D., and Ph.D., author of *Power vs. Force*, believe that this discipline offers access to both the individual subconscious and the collective unconscious.

For example try this while saying your name truthfully and then falsely. The key here is that you must ask yourself clear, "yes" or "no" questions.

Inner sense development is a discipline to which we all seem to be headed. We are born with these latent abilities, but must practice to gain proficiency. The constant challenge is to awaken to these realms at one's own pace.

The lag factor

After receiving a strong intuitive signal, how long will it take to get results? Will it happen at all? That is, can your Partners execute? Or will they? If they can't or won't execute it, why not? How are you going to stay in touch? If you start down a path of complete trust and faith, how far will you have to go before you receive assurances you are on the right trail?

You will have to stay open to your intuition, be willing to give it more attention, and then act on it.

If you start down this path how are you going to know you are not on a wild goose chase? "Synchronicities" and feeling "in the flow" will validate that you are on the right path. Positive and negative synchronicities are the contact efforts of your Invisible Partners.

Synchronicity is a term coined by Jung that refers to meaningful coincidences — that is, events connected, but not by cause and effect. For example, suppose you are thinking about calling a friend and at that same moment the phone rings and it is that friend. This is not a mere coincidence, but a meaningful coincidence. It means that there is a piece of information to harvest from the conversation.

Let's say that the friend was calling to tell you that there was art exhibit she thought you might be interested in attending the next evening. On the way to the exhibit, at the show, or returning from it you'll receive a useful piece of information from your Invisible Partners. It may be from a personal contact, or something you see, read or hear.

Your first decision would be whether to go or not. If you do not go, your Invisible Partners will have to try again. If you go, your antennae will be up. Being aware of this, you should try to alter your schedule so that synchronicities take priority.

Let's look at a few more examples to make synchronicities more familiar.

You are wrestling with an issue at the office. You are debating whether to support or oppose it. On the way home you decide to run an errand but are not sure exactly which street to take. You find yourself on a street with your exact same last name. This would be a synchronicity. However the street dead-ends. You cannot get through. This would be a negative synchronicity. It would be a cautionary flag around supporting the issue at the office.

You and your wife are planning a vacation. She wants to go to Europe and you want to go to South America. You are at the office. You get up to take a break, walk down the hallway, and someone has a radio on. The commercial at that exact moment is touting that there is no better time to travel to Europe.

You are at a restaurant and are debating whether to have fish or that big steak. Your cholesterol levels are a bit high, but this is a celebration. You rationalize and order the steak, but at that very moment another waiter passes by with the fish dish you were in debate over. It looks good. You change your order on the spot.

You have signed a contract to make the biggest home purchase of your life, but you have not closed yet, and you could back out. Your intuition tells you it is right, but your rational mind is throwing up caution flags. Your dog brings you the paper. As you open it up, the front page features a story on how now is the best time to buy a home.

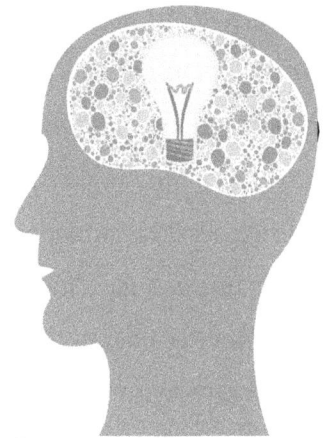

Learning More: Recalling Synchronicities

When Sandy was diagnosed with prostate cancer, he was in that vulnerable state of wondering how to deal with a life-threatening and scary proposition. The urologist scheduled him for an appointment to discuss surgery. His gut told him this was not for him.

Just before he went into see the doctor he picked up the latest issue of Scientific American. *In it was an article on the reliability of a prostatectomy, the removal of the entire prostate gland. It said there was a 35 to 40% failure rate.*

He told the urologist he wasn't going to have the surgery.

Eleven years later he still hasn't had the surgery, nor anything else for that matter — just annual scans to let him know how he is faring.

Here's another example.

When Sandy set out to purchase his first house in Honolulu, the broker found a home high up in the mountains overlooking Honolulu. The house didn't have a view and was situated down a steep drive, but he was anxious to make an offer. The house price was close to $100,000. Through the broker Sandy made two offers and one counter-offer. He was $300 away from a deal. The seller wouldn't budge. The broker could have thrown in the $300 and the deal would have gone through. Instead she said, "This house just isn't for you." A week later the broker got a call from a doctor who had bought a house through her four years earlier. He was moving, and he was selling. The broker called Sandy and they went to look at the house before it was even listed. It was perfect — beyond words. Sandy placed an offer and it was immediately accepted. It was a sanctuary during his entire advertising career. Thirty years later he still owns the home.

A word about positive synchronicities leading to what look like negative outcomes: you would think this might be a contradiction. Just because an immediate event does not turn out as you had hoped does not mean that you have been steered in the wrong direction. An initial loss or setback may just be paving the way for something much better. There is a story that noted author, lecturer and physician Dr. Bernie Siegel tells. He had rented a car and was returning it to the airport. He was the featured speaker at a large conference. On the way his car had a flat tire. Having missed the plane he was frustrated and angry. That plane he missed crashed, killing everyone aboard. He returned to rental car company and asked if they would give him the tire. It now hangs in his house, bronzed.

Recall up to seven total synchronicities, at least one of which was a negative one. See if you can remember what the synchronicity led you to do. How did it work out? Note: There are little things that happen all the time. It is probably difficult to remember them, because they fade away like dreams. The larger synchronicities are attached to major life-changing situations and are more easily recalled.

Describe synchronicity #1:

What did it lead you to do?

How did it work out?

Describe synchronicity #2:

What did it lead you to do?

How did it work out?

Describe synchronicity #3:

What did it lead you to do?

How did it work out?

Describe synchronicity #4:

What did it lead you to do?

How did it work out?

Describe synchronicity #5:

What did it lead you to do?

How did it work out?

Describe synchronicity #6:

What did it lead you to do?

How did it work out?

Describe synchronicity #7:

What did it lead you to do?

How did it work out?

Now answer these questions about this exercise.

What have I learned from this exercise?

Where are my opportunities?

What actions will I take?

When Things Are Not Happening

There are numerous desires that do not come about. What are the counter-forces? Perhaps you want to win a contest. There can only be one winner. Your opponent may have prepared and wants it more than you.

Perhaps many are aligned against you. You want a social change, but there is great opposition. If your goals in life become feelings, then setbacks in the outer world are merely challenges to overcome. If your intuition tells you that you are on the right path then patience and persistence will serve you. Keep looking for synchronicities to assure yourself you still are on course.

It is said that Christopher Columbus petitioned Queen Isabella for seven years to no avail. She would not see him. Ready to give up, he met a priest by the name of Perez and told him of his vision, trials and tribulations. It turned out Perez was the priest to Queen Isabella. He put in a good word and the rest is history.

What other factors are affecting the outcome? Are your desires masking a fear so that it is the fear that is being ordered rather than the thing itself? For example what if you want a promotion, but are obsessed with the fear that you are not good enough? The real message you are putting out is that you should not have the promotion because you are not qualified.

Upping the ante and the nature of fear

This is an exceptionally important area and one not to take lightly. There is a plethora of advice on how to overcome fear. Certain fears are a necessary part of our survival hard-wiring. We don't touch the red-hot burner on the stove with our fingers. Yet we can learn how to walk on hot coals with the proper instruction. We usually find a coach if it is something difficult. We model, practice and slowly work our way up. Whether in sports, medicine, financial management, or other areas requiring the development of skill sets, there is a slow step-by-step process leading eventually to mastery.

For this discussion we are not addressing fear from creatures in the wild, or daredevil feats, but fears of possible event outcomes in the future.

In the intuitive realm, where we have been using the paradigm of communication with our Invisible Partners, we have stressed that one's intentions need to be for pure experiences. If you really want the thrill of becoming a jet pilot, acting on Broadway, being a surgeon etc., there will be fearful moments, but you'll be in alignment with your Invisible Partners and moving through the steps necessary for success.

We have also discussed ways to practice being in touch with your Invisible Partners. The parking spot or elevator door opening just as you need it, or the plane being delayed as you run to make it, seem to be just luck — as if you had nothing to do with these events happening. There is not much at stake if these events do not occur. Yet if you do see the connection you will then consciously feel more confident about raising the ante.

Yet as the ante goes up there is more concern for the outcome, because we see things in terms of how hard we have worked to acquire them. If we take an unnecessary risk and things go badly, we lose and perhaps have to start over.

This is particularly true with the investment of money. We are tempted to sometimes gamble. Yet why are we gambling? What is it that we are hoping for? Maybe it is the desire for a windfall that will then relieve us of the need for future efforts. Yet for us this approach discounts the potential magic our Invisible Partners can create for us as we truly need it. <u>Gambling undermines our own personal power</u>. This is the alligator with which we all wrestle.

Another example, and one many of us have experienced, is the urge to uproot and move to an entirely new location. We have to quit our job, and leave our familiar connections of friends and family. Having made the commitment, we go. As we do, things fall into place. Maybe not all at once, but eventually the job break or right relationship comes about. We may not give our thought and desire patterns any credence, but we have created orders and our Invisible Partners have been helping.

We have also pointed out that at times there may be an inspired idea which comes to you from out of the blue, such as the one Sandy had to build a collection of Frank Lloyd Wright's un-built designs. Here, after the initial "aha," he began to follow inner guidance, trusting that the right people would show up to make it happen. He did not have development experience, and seasoned investors could not really have been expected to give him money even though he was asking for it. But when experienced developers showed up wanting to incorporate this idea into theirs, it was the perfect solution. He just had to have the perseverance to continue on.

Prior to these developers showing up, Sandy had one great moment of truth. He had convinced Signal Oil to give him an option on 450 acres on the island of Hawaii. This was used to create a master plan demonstrating how seventy-five actual Frank Lloyd Wright homes could be built there. They eventually required him to commit to buying the property for $1.9 million. He would not have to come up with the money for a year, but then payments would be required. He had no way of making many of those payments, yet he felt that he had to go through with it. Although failure would have bankrupted him, he believed he was in alignment with his Invisible Partners. He had been training and slowly upping the ante. This was his moment of truth. He committed: he metaphorically jumped off of the cliff.

Yet, if our desires are for something to mask a deep rooted insecurity or fear, then we have to be careful that we are not deluding ourselves or brainwashing ourselves into taking risks that are not supported by our Invisible Partners.

In the example we just mentioned, Sandy's attorney finally stopped him from signing the land-purchase contract. His willingness was honest commitment enough, and his attorney's actions were also motivated from a deep inner feeling. Sandy felt relieved and empty at the same time. In the end, the project launched in Maui. If Sandy had bought the Hawaii Island land, he would have had an unnecessary land obligation. You could say that his Partners were ultimately working in his interest.

Peeling the onion

The way this works is to examine a fear, then track it by "peeling" away each fear until you no longer feel fear's emotional grip. At that point you can say to yourself, "Yeah, I can live with that."

Maybe the biggest fear you have is losing the income to make a mortgage payment. We'll go through a hypothetical peel.

First peel: What's so bad about not being able to make the payment? You will lose your house.

Second peel: What's so bad about losing the house? You won't have a place to live since you don't have a job.

Third peel: What's so bad about losing a place to live? You would feel the shame of failure and have to bunk with friends or family.

Fourth peel: What's so bad about temporarily bunking up with friends or family until you get back on your feet? Isn't failure really a part of life that everyone experiences? <u>Somewhere the fear loses its energy because you can live with this as the worst outcome.</u> Maybe you'll develop new relationships and ways to see things you could not imagine before the crisis.

The purpose of this exercise is to free ourselves from the unresourceful state. It is difficult to be exercising a sense of power and sending intense orders to the universe via our Invisible Partners if we feel totally unempowered.

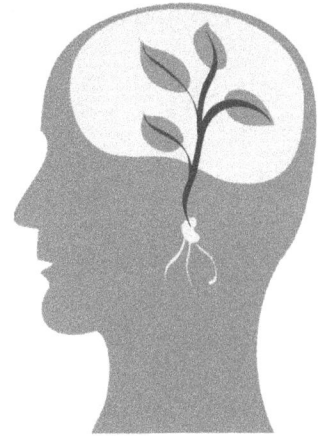

Learning More: Onion-Peeling

Pick your greatest fear. Go through the peel process. Peel until the fear loses its grip on you.

Describe what you fear.

What's so bad about that?

What's so bad about that?

What's so bad about that?

Do you feel more resourceful about this fear now? You may want to turn to the back of the book and take a couple of pages to go through the same exercise with other fears.

Now answer these questions about this exercise.

What have I learned from this exercise?

Where are my opportunities?

What actions will I take?

Other Factors Affecting the Outcome: Staying "On Purpose"

When we are moving through life and have tapped into a purposeful vein, we can feel the energy supporting our endeavors. We have the energy to keep pushing in a certain direction. When we waver, we can feel the energy subside. Oscar Wilde once said, "I can avoid anything but temptation." We take detours or follow the drumbeat of some other person because we want to be accepted, or we want to accommodate friends, or we rationalize the choice. The small items become invisible in life, but a pattern can form which sabotages our bigger dreams. Perhaps we want to be better at a life skill, or hobby, or a new endeavor, but each time we get down to it there is interference or some "other thing" that comes up. When it comes time to take that courageous step for the big chance or opportunity, we may let it pass us by because we are so used to the pattern. All of the help our Invisible Partners might have been able to bring us vanishes. If sometimes we follow our inner guidance and sometimes we don't, the lag time may become so long, we cannot possibly connect the original desire and intention to the outcome.

As we become conscious about manifesting our desires and intentions, the bar seems to be raised. We draw bigger assignments to ourselves with greater potential. The feedback loop allows us to see that we have increasingly more power.

In his book, Sandy writes about SHOOSOX, a novelty idea that popped into his head one afternoon at the height of the Pet Rock and Shower Mike era. He had running shoes, wing tips and sneakers silkscreened onto tube socks and packaged in little shoe-boxes.

Sandy had designs patented and samples and displays made, and then struck out to take orders, not knowing what pitfalls were in store. The moment of truth came when he had to invest 50% up-front for the production of the socks. He needed to fill existing orders, not knowing if the socks would be manufactured in time to meet the narrow Christmas delivery window.

At the last moment the J.P. Stevens Company stepped in, took a license, and paid him enough to cover all of his expenses. He returned to Hawaii, having been away from the agency for two months. He had set out, not knowing how or where it would end, but trusting that it would work out. <u>It felt right, and when he reflected on it later he realized it had been a laboratory experiment in conscious manifestation.</u>

Following our deepest passions does not mean that we abandon our responsibilities, or that our passionate desires will come easy. However, we have a direction and the energy to move us there.

Learning More: How Close Are You to Being "On Purpose?"

Write yourself a make-believe check for all of the money you could ever want.

The check amount is for $_____.

You are now completely free to do anything you want.

Write a brief description of the life you are leading now (before the check) and your feelings regarding what is keeping you stuck (if indeed you are stuck.)

Now, after the big cash infusion, write a description of the new life you are leading, the one that allows you to follow your bliss. What are your feelings?

How big a difference is there between your two lives? Is it mostly a matter of degree, or are your two lives profoundly different? If they are profoundly different, you now have a clearer picture of your heart's desire. You now know your direction and desired feelings. Make a short list of actions you can take to begin. If that is not easily done, then focus on desired feelings with intent.

Now answer these questions about this exercise.

What have I learned from this exercise?

Where are my opportunities?

What actions will I take?

Other Factors Affecting the Outcome:
Kindness Versus Harm, and Ethical Decision-Making

As you have seen, this workbook is not only about new ways to manifest, but also an examination of what to want. Years ago Sandy was in a small presentation in San Francisco where the Dalai Lama was answering questions about his own philosophy of life. <u>He said that he practiced kindness to all sentient beings because it distorted reality the least</u>. (He also said he would perhaps make an exception for the mosquito.)

Sandy spent time with his answer, and realized that if kindness permeates our thoughts, kindness is the world we will create. It is a much more soul-enriching experience than its counterpart. If you create harm, cruelty and callousness, your world will mirror this to you. Fear, paranoia, revenge, mistrust, hate, violence and suffering will permeate your new reality. <u>This is a much more challenging existence to manage, especially when we are living in such rapidly changing times.</u> Think of the effort it takes to lie, cover up, deceive and keep wrongness sustained.

A friend of Sandy's said to him one day that he makes it a habit to perform one kind act a day for somebody as an investment in the idea.

Ethical decision-making

As time speeds up like it or not we are being forced to develop means of cooperating to survive. More and more we simply have to trust. Social networking is revealing shabby products, services, and actions. Transparency is leveling the field.

From this viewpoint our inner compass can give us an ethical read on any situation. Ethics is controversial because it has so many filters and lenses. However, our observation is that we all have a moral compass appropriate to our times. It is tempered by our cultural influences, our inner programming from birth, and the evolutionary changes the world brings. It is a dynamic. What might have been an acceptable view at one time no longer is now. For example not long ago there was a true belief that some races were favored over others. Now there is an acceptance that wisdom resides everywhere and that individuals and groups have chosen to have different experiences. Is one experience better than another? Who can judge? Yet, as we individually and collectively experience pain, in whatever form, our tendency is to remember and avoid it in the future.

Our world is morphing into increasing interconnectedness: climate is changing, pollution is exported, communication is instant, and life at all levels is becoming more transparent and honest. In this kind of world there is a need to make sure all of the parts are eventually brought up to speed. Do our decisions support or resist this rapidly unfolding broad sweep? As the philosopher Alfred North Whitehead observed, the universe seems to be made up of two opposing forces: novelty and habit. Habit is the status quo – the preservation of what is comfortable and familiar. Novelty is the relentless process of change. There is always more novelty than habit.

A Quick Review

So far we have been discussing that as the ante increases and we consciously step into greater manifestation awareness, there are useful guidelines to follow. If we just want things or people in our lives as a means to something else, why not try to identify what that something else is? That's what we really want in the first place. It is usually a feeling of some kind. If we make that feeling the goal, then our Invisible Partners and the universe have a wider range of choices to explore for us.

If our objectives are pure experiences, such as to own something well made, or to be in the company of certain people, or to master some endeavor, then we are aligning ourselves in the most efficient way with forces that can help us.

If we are fearful, drawn to paths that are not purposeful or ethical, or that are harmful to others, then we get outcomes — but not necessarily the desired ones. In this new world we are moving into, our desires and intentions are manifesting much quicker.

We have to trust our intuition more and more. Yet in so doing we are learning that the map of that territory has a structure also. Our urges and inner guidance point us in a direction, and the synchronicities in our lives can tell us whether we are on the right path for ourselves.

So far we have discussed the ideas and concerns for structuring our lives so that we can more effectively know what to want and how to obtain it. Yet there is another side of the equation that makes life even more exciting.

What do your Partners want?

This takes us to the flip side of the coin. In the paradigm we have been discussing we have been looking at how to give our Invisible Partners effective orders. That is, we have stuff we want them to do.

Since this is a partnership, a two-way street, what about ideas they might have?

They need our cooperation in the material world. They need our arms and legs to do the footwork. <u>We like to think that when we receive a great idea, insight, sudden flash, or a strong urge to do something, perhaps these are coming from our Invisible Partners</u>.

Are you the only one being given an idea? Who knows? Maybe many people's Invisible Partners are sending the same messages in hopes that somebody will pay attention. We are not only living our individual lives, but are living part of a much grander scheme — one that is constantly revealing itself.

For example, maybe if you pay attention to a sudden desire to turn a certain direction and walk down a particular street, you will meet someone that you need to or that you wanted to meet, or maybe you'll find some small thing you have been searching for.

The reason is really unimportant. We only have to trust that it is a mission that will be in our best interest and that will support us if we listen, and follow the leads and signposts along the way. What is important is that we are making the connections. We are getting used to recognizing patterns. Whether they are intuitive signals or synchronistic signs along the way, it doesn't really matter. The more we feel a part of what is around us, the more we feel the dance. That it comes is all that is important.

The idea is to take note of small coincidences. They reinforce our belief system. And the more we believe the more we see and experience. Some people use intuitive skills to garner useful coincidences. As this framework starts to develop, it will become more certain, just like the linear one to which we have all become accustomed.

What is so important is this:

- Ordinary life can become extraordinary. A trip to the mall or a bookstore taken as a result of an intuitive feeling heightens our senses; it opens us to the possibilities of new directions through potential meetings or information.

- Time may no longer be a constraint. Rather than having to plan how resources will slowly build through a step-by-step methodology, they might show up in the most unsuspecting manner.

Sandy's book is titled *How Frank Lloyd Wright Got Into My Head, Under My Skin,*

And Changed the Way I Think About Thinking because it details a step on his journey of learning new ways to manifest. It's a big step. For Sandy, Frank Lloyd Wright and those who lived around him served as catalysts.

Never before had Sandy risked everything. He had to wrestle with all of the issues we have discussed in this workbook. Was he doing it for money or was he doing it for the joy of the experience and accepting that whatever the returns, they would be appropriate? Could he face bankruptcy and start all over again?

The idea of building a collection of Frank Lloyd Wright's designs was intoxicating for Sandy. At some level he felt not only called, but also compelled. Although he had no real development experience, he felt as if the manifestation process itself was summoning him. He had been exposed to real pioneers living and breathing these ideas. He had been slowly studying and sampling. It was simply time. There were numerous synchronicities surrounding the idea, all of which he describes in detail in the book. The right people seemed to appear.

The subhead, *A Creative Thinking Blueprint for the 21st Century,* is very appropriate for the book, because when we begin to trust our intuition and look for synchronicities as communiqués, we enter a new arena: it is a team effort. There is two-way communication. We may not know who all the team players are, but they are there. It is an easier and more logical matter to accept the idea that a wonderful insight has come from some consciousness somewhere rather than from nowhere. Once you act on that insight, it will be as if you picked up the ball and now it is in play. Is the big idea you receive the final goal, an enticement, or part of a larger picture that reveals itself as you take action?

In this last calling to build these Frank Lloyd Wright designs, ideas, people and synchronicities propelled Sandy along a certain path. He was focused on building a collection. Yet it didn't turn out that way; or, at least, it hasn't yet.

What did result was tapestry of rich experiences. Sandy met and worked with fascinating people. He was exposed to some of the great art forms on the American landscape. The project secured a large architectural commission for the Frank Lloyd Wright Foundation and left a stunning building on the Maui landscape. None of his small group lost any money.

In the second part of the adventure he had the rare experience of building one of the original homes. Like magic, the home almost built itself. It cost at least three times more than all of the estimates, but the money showed up almost miraculously as it was needed. True craftsmen appeared. Mistakes turned into blessings. When it was completed, it became a portal for hosting luminaries who exemplified life on the edge. They were all controversial people straddling the fine divide between acceptable social norms and new thinking patterns.

Along the way Sandy experienced divorce and cancer. Yet when this part of his journey was over, the rewards were more than he could have ever imagined. Yes, there was profit in the sale of the house, but much more importantly he had learned what forgiveness and non-judgment truly meant, and had come to trust in this new partnership. In that regard he found himself willing to follow some of the "wildest ideas," like using the Institute for Resonance Therapy in Germany to help sell the house.

Our journeys can be thought of as joint efforts with our Invisible Partners. We may have one thing in mind in the beginning, and our Partners, something else. As we open to the partnership we can be led to rewarding experiences beyond anything we could have ever imagined.

Accepting and nurturing this relationship means consciously opening ourselves to the rich fabric of another realm. Like learning another language it requires mindfulness, attunement, and the willingness to act on these communiqués.

Getting Into the Flow

As this begins to be part of our life we enter the realm of being "in the flow." "Flow" is a term that has been popularized in the western world by psychologist Mihaly Csikszentmihalyi; it refers to a state of focused motivation. Here we harness our emotions in such a way that energy flows through us, aligning with the task at hand in a perfectly balanced manner. We feel as if we are not just doing it, but <u>are the doing</u>. Athletes often refer to this state as being in the zone.

In the context we have been discussing, the idea of flowing with our Invisible Partners makes the entire process of life a flow. It means that we move intuitively and consciously through our day recognizing any synchronicity (positive or negative) as a signal that we are in touch with our Partners.

In the flow of the day each intuitive decision that we make becomes instantaneous and seamless. Yet these decisions follow a path.

The Sims Method: new criteria for creative thinking and decision-making about contemplated action

The importance of decision-making has never been greater as we experience a mind-altering sensation of time compression. Intuitive training and strategies are essential to the role of decision-making as a matter of survival in the 21st century. The objective is to develop intuitive confidence matching that of our more linear decision-making model. To accomplish this, the process will have to incorporate a new model of decision-making.

Set your goal for the "best outcome for all concerned" as relates to the action contemplated. If you are making decisions in a group, think of it as harvesting the group mind by aligning the group creative thinking process. This intention is a foundation order to your ultimate team, your Invisible Partners.

Evaluate the action contemplated through a values screen. Is it ethical? Is it purposeful? Is it harmful? Is it in line with your core values? If not, stop. Consider a new action.

You need to practice consciously using the same decision-making process in both low-risk and high-risk situations. This will hone your skills, much as diving skills are improved incrementally from low board to high board.

As you move up the risk continuum, evaluate the nature of the desire or objective. Is it for a pure experience or is it masking a fear? A pure experience would be obtaining a goal for the sheer joy of it, such as building a better product, one that lasts or is easier to use. Masking a fear implies that the objective is to gain an outcome to prevent some fear from occurring. That is, the fear inadvertently may replace the ultimate goal. The fear becomes the projection to your Invisible Partners as well as what you request. It is a diluted request. If the action is masking, then stop. Consider a new action.

Now check your intuition. If you get a "no" then stop. Consider a new action. If you get a "yes," then proceed until you: (1) get a successful outcome, or (2) a negative outcome. A negative outcome may not necessarily be bad. It may simply cause a new and better course of action.

There is the story of the Chinese peasant whose prized horse escapes. His neighbor says to him, "Oh, what a tragedy." The peasant says, "Maybe so, maybe not." The peasant sends his son out to recover the horse riding a mule. The son falls off and breaks a leg, but recovers the horse. The neighbor says, "Oh what a tragedy." The peasant says, "Maybe so, maybe not." The next day the Chinese army sweeps through the village, conscripting every able-bodied young man. The peasant's son is spared.

Before having an outcome you may experience synchronicities. These are meetings between inner desires and outer world occurrences. If the synchronicity is positive, keep proceeding. If it is negative, then either stop and consider a new action or continue on until you receive a confirming second negative synchronicity. In that case, stop and consider a new action.

Harnessing your intuition by practicing low levels of risk and documenting the feedback will provide you with the confidence to accept greater degrees of uncertainty.

Consciously embracing this creates more confidence in the process and provides you a more tested and creative way to approach the unknown.

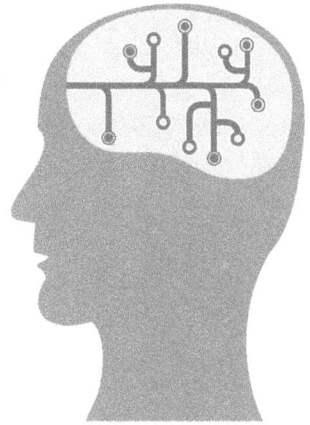

Learning More: A Continuous Journal of Daily Synchronicities, Intuitive Urges, and Revelations

This exercise is like getting results in a gym. Start by recognizing and recording intuitive urges, synchronicities, and your own revelations. The process should build on itself. As you become more aware, the process should produce increasingly more synchronicities. If you are facing intense life challenges, this process should produce even greater numbers of synchronicities.

As you proceed, notice how your entire day feels. Do you feel more connected? Do you feel more like you are on a team than before? Do you feel that you are on the right path? Do you feel that you are getting in the flow of life? Did you have anything particularly significant happen?

You might want to observe that as time goes by, and as you increase your exposure to new environments and situations, the frequency of synchronicities should increase. In other words signs of certainty will begin to appear in uncertain territory.

The Nissan automobile commercials used to say, "Life is a journey — enjoy the ride." The ideas put forth here will help you do just that.

Notes on synchronicity:

Summary

We are living in watershed times. Massive change is upon us from all sides. Technology is moving at warp speed. Worldwide financial and currency markets are unstable. The environment is threatened. Cultural differences are dissolving... all of this in the blink of a cosmic eye. What we are morphing into is not yet clear. But we can acquire new tools and assistance.

We live in a richer interconnected universal fabric than we may have imagined. What appears to be chance, coincidence, and luck seems to be part of a larger order. Intuition may be as concrete as our linear brain associations, but we have not mastered that state yet.

While we give credence to unseen forces, forging new working relationships and communication techniques seems to not only be possible but a requirement in the times ahead.

This workbook suggests ideas for how to adapt and optimize life patterns.

The ideas stressed were:

- Knowing what to want is at the core. The quality of your life is truly determined by the questions you ask.

- Getting what you want is a matter of recognizing your own personal power and how to effectively employ it. Set your desires with strong intent, revel in the feeling of having achieved the goal, release with thanks, and accept that it will happen if it is meant to.

- Making feelings your goals will address the core desires of much of what you want.

- Partnering with unseen forces can be thought about in more familiar terms — buddies, or pals, or ones you can count on. They have the vision: you have the arms and legs. Synchronicities, and perhaps your "great aha experiences," are their way of communicating.

- Harnessing their help improves if your desires are ethical, kind in intent, and purposeful; if your desires are for pure experiences and not masking fears; and if your desires feel intuitively good.

- Failing to reach a desired outcome may not be as catastrophic as it first appears. The failure may be setting the stage for something much better or appropriate.

Hopefully this workbook will have given you a fresh point of view, new thought patterns to practice, associations to recognize, and tools to employ in optimizing your life experiences in the coming years of rapid change.

Sandy Sims and Kerry Monick, 2011

Suggested Readings, Films, Lectures

The resources set forth below comprise a diverse sample from a wide variety of sources. Some are from science and others from the cusp or "soon to be science." And finally there is the robust Seth material, channeled by Jane Roberts, which is simply beyond imagination and has been likened to talking with someone with an I.Q. of 400. The samplings are to stimulate and encourage thought, trial and your own observations.

Orientation

Russell, Peter. *Waking Up In Time: Finding Inner Peace In Times of Accelerating Change.* Novato: Origin Press, 2007.

Yatri. *Unknown Man: The Mysterious Birth of a New Species.* New York: Fireside, 1988.

Nature of the field

Hawkins, Dr. David R. *Power vs. Force: The Hidden Determinants of Human Behavior.* Carlsbad: Hay House, 2004.

McTaggart, Lynne. *The Field: The Quest for the Secret Force of the Universe.* Brattleboro: Harper Paperbacks, 2008.

Mitchell, Dr. Edgar. *Global Mind Change.*

Sheldrake, Rupert. *Morphic Resonance: The Nature of Formative Causation.* Rochester: Park Street Press, 2009.

Talbot, Michael. *The Holographic Universe.* New York: Harper Perennial, 1992.

What the Bleep!? - Down the Rabbit Hole. 20th Century Fox, 2006. DVD.

Who we are

Roberts, Jane. *Seth Speaks: The Eternal Validity of the Soul.* San Rafael: Amber-Allen Publishing, 1994.

Roberts, Jane, and Seth. *Dreams, "Evolution" and Value Fulfillment, Vol. 2: A Seth Book.* San Rafael: Amber-Allen Publishing, 1997.

— *The "Unknown" Reality, Vol. 1: A Seth Book.* San Rafael: Amber-Allen Publishing, 1997.

— *The Individual and the Nature of Mass Events: A Seth Book.* San Rafael: Amber-Allen Publishing, 1995.

Knowing what to want

Belitz, Charlene, and Meg Lundstrom. *The Power of Flow: Practical Ways to Transform Your Life with Meaningful Coincidence.* New York: Three Rivers Press, 1998.

Bolen, Jean Shinoda. *The Tao of Psychology: Synchronicity and Self.* San Francisco: HarperSanFrancisco, 1982.

Campbell, Joseph. *The Hero's Journey: Joseph Campbell on His Life and Work.* Novato: New World Library, 2003.

Csikszentmihalyi, Mihaly. *Flow: The Psychology of Optimal Experience.* New York: Harper Perennial Modern Classics, 2007.

— *The Evolving Self.* New York: Harper Perennial, 1994.

Robbins, Anthony. *Awaken the Giant Within.* New York: Simon & Schuster, 1992.

Purposefulness path

Campbell, Joseph. *The Hero with a Thousand Faces.* Novato: New World Library, 2008.

Houston, Jean. *A Mythic Life: Learning to Live our Greater Story.* New York: Harperone, 1996.

— *Jump Time: Shaping Your Future in a World of Radical Change.* Boulder: Sentient Publications, 2004.

Leonard, George. *Mastery: The Keys to Success and Long-Term Fulfillment.* New York: Plume, 1992.

Millman, Dan. *The Life You Were Born to Live: A Guide to Finding Your Life Purpose.* San Francisco: HJ Kramer, 1995.

Redfield, James and Carol Adrienne. *The Celestine Prophecy: An Experiential Guide.* New York: Grand Central Publishing, 1995.

Spangler, David. *The Call.* Boston: Riverhead Trade, 1998.

New ways to manifest

Holmes, Ernest and Michael Beckwith. *How to Change Your Life: An Inspirational, Life-Changing Classic from the Ernest Holmes Library.* Deerfield Beach: HCI, 1999.

McTaggart, Lynne. *The Intention Experiment: Using Your Thoughts to Change Your Life and the World.* New York City: Free Press, 2008.

Spangler, David. *Everyday Miracles: the Inner Art of Manifestation.* Harvard University: Lorian Press, 2008.

— *The Laws of Manifestation: A Consciousness Classic.* San Francisco: Weiser Books, 2009.

About the Authors

Reginald Sanderson (Sandy) Sims was raised and educated in the South. After serving as Naval Officer and finishing graduate business school, he followed a dream to live in Honolulu, where he built one of Hawaii's largest and most successful advertising agencies. He resides in Hawaii and San Miguel de Allende, Mexico.

Kerry Monick, MD, grew up in Perth, Western Australia and upon graduating at UWA in Medicine, also followed her dream to Hawaii, where she studied psychiatry and was based for 20 years. Post-graduate university studies continued in London and New York. She embraces a metaphysical world view alongside the conventional and continues to live with a foot in both camps. She has practiced psychiatry with neurofeedback and nutritional techniques and is currently in private practice in Perth.

www.ingramcontent.com/pod-product-compliance
Lightning Source LLC
Chambersburg PA
CBHW081936110426
42742CB00040BA/3215